FIVE-BOOKS-IN-ONE

Change Your Destiny

How to get paid appearing in TV Ads and Soapies

100's of Opportunities for you to make money

Expert Telemarketing: How to urgently get lots of sales appointments

Get paid for the poems you write

Change Your Destiny

By Bernard Levine

If you are unhappy and believe in your heart that you truly deserve a better life….

If you are wanting to elevate your life to a higher position….

When you are fed up and sick and tired of struggling, battling to survive….

When you feel your life is in a rut going nowhere….

It is only then…

It is only when you have reached that point in your life

How to Get Paid and Start Earning a Good Income

By Bernard Levine

And now for some good news....

No more worrying about money!

How are you going to put food on the table?

How will you pay all your bills?

How will you keep your head above water?

You deserve a better life now and a new tomorrow.

This special unique edition of 5-books-in-one will help you earn a living and put money into your bank account.

And don't let nobody stop you!

The ideas and opportunities in this volume of books are immense!

Remember, you don't have to stick with one job...

Yes, you can now have two, three and even more income streams providing you with money all at the same time!

It's not where you start, but where you finish! If you are looking for an additional income, there's lots here too!

Read this book very carefully, make notes, follow and go for it!!!

Your life will never be the same!

when you are really unhappy and dissatisfied with the circumstances of your life…
the way that things have been going and turning out…
that you will get out of your comfort zone to take action and do something about changing your life.

If you are now ready to stand up, give yourself a better life and move forward, then this book will be your lifesaver to take your life onto a fast success track.

Follow your heart to the things that will make you happy and embark on a life path you will be proud of.
Let the good times begin for YOU!

There's a saying that says: When life hands you a lemon, you've got to make lemonade!

To get your life onto a success track and go forward, you've got to have a workable plan of action.

You've got to have realistic goals that you can aim towards achieving …things in your life that you want to improve, something to strive for, change and achieve.

You got to do something useful with your life….not just hang around and exist!

So, what should you do…

Firstly, let's imagine that I am a fairy godmother and I'm going to give you any 3 wishes you would like to see come true.

But, you have got to follow the rules…

Rule number one is you are not allowed to wish for money….
and rule number two is you cannot wish for more wishes.
That's right! You've only got 3 wishes.

Now, tell me, what are the 3 wishes you would like to see happen and come true for yourself?
What will make you happy?
Where do you want to be?
What's your purpose in life?
What do you want to achieve?
What are your goals?
How are you going to get there?
Have you written down any plans?

These are some life-changing questions you should ask yourself…
Why are you here?
What am I doing with my life?
What do I want?
Where am I going?

You must define and decide exactly what you want.
It's no good saying "I want to be happy" or "I want to be successful."

Your goals must be specific, definite and not be vague.
Realize that your definition of what happiness means to you, could be totally different to what happiness means to someone else.
For example, for a golfer happiness could be to win a major golf tournament …however to a talented pop singer, happiness might be recording her first album.

Secrets of Winning
Aim for a specific goal – put blinkers on and go for it!

Believe in yourself – your talents, skills and abilities.
Have a strong burning desire to win and succeed.
Prayer is the strongest form of energy – use it!
Keep your life simple, well-disciplined and organized.
Check your progress regularly.
Success in life depends on confidence and enthusiasm.
Be hungry! Be desperate! Be determined to succeed.
What you put into life is what you will get out of life.
You make your own success!

Let's look at what you really want out of life.
What are your needs?
What do you desire most in life?
What is important to you?
What do you value most in life?

What will truly make you happy?
What would you place as your number 1
priority at the very top of your list?

Write down:
All the things you want to have
All the places you want to go
All the things you want to be
All the things you want to know
All the things you want to do.

If you have a goal in life
That takes a lot of energy
That incurs a great deal of interest
And that is a challenge to you,
You will always look
forward to waking up to
see what the new day brings.
Author unknown

To have all-round complete fulfilment in your life, you need to have different goals for different specific areas of your life.
Are you looking for fame and fortune?
How important is financial security to you?
What do you want to do for your family?

Always Have a Dream

Follow your heart

to the path of greatness

that lies within you.

The secret of life

is to have something

to look forward to

everyday.

Find a dream that excites you
and make plans
of how you are going
to achieve it.

Feed your mind daily
with positive energy
and words of inspiration.
Take your life to a higher level.
Stay focused and go forward
with your eyes on the prize.
When you run towards your destination
with passion in your heart
you will see your dreams come true.

Ideally, you should have short term and long term goals.

Your short term goals for certain projects could be say, 6 months….while your long term goals could be 1 year or more. I want you now to make a list of your short and long term goals. What would you like to achieve in 6 months time and later on in 1 year or more.

When you have no goals, you will find that whichever way the wind blows and whatever life throws at you …it will take hold of your life and you will just be pulled along and drift aimlessly without any direction or sense of purpose.

But, when you set meaningful and worthwhile goals for yourself that you want to achieve, you will have a firm foundation and a path to point you in the right direction to self-fulfilment.

And every time you accomplish your goal, you will feel a sense of joy and satisfaction.

Achieving what you set out to do, is very rewarding and exciting.
Work out a plan of action and decide what is it that you need to do to achieve your goals.
Then, follow your plan of action and all the steps you need to take to attain your dreams.

Secrets of Success

You are the architect of your life
Create your own opportunities
and make things happen.
Set yourself a specific goal
and monitor your progress.
Be of service
Keep doing things for others
without counting the cost.
Turn your defeats into victories
Control your environment.
Mix with the kind of
people who inspire you.
Keep your attitude positive
and your health in fine trim.
Let God go before you

in everything you do.

Pray regularly with feeling.

Always be planning

something constantly.

You are the magnet of

your circumstances.

Never give up!

Now, what are the type of specific goals, you should be writing down?
Should you just focus on having one main priority goal?

When you focus on just one goal, it does not take into account your whole being of who you really are, your entire make-up of all the various aspects of your life.

Yes, I believe that you should have one main priority goal, but you should also have several other less important goals which you would like to see come true.

After all, is chasing wealth and acquiring possessions really your prime and only focus in life?

If you are just going to concentrate on making money as your main function and purpose in life, then you will be neglecting all the other dimensions of fulfilling a richer and more rewarding purpose.

Secrets of Happiness

Kindness is the most

beautiful jewel in the world.

Love means having consideration
for each other.
The seeds you sow today
will be your fruit of tomorrow.
Fill your day with prayer
and your life with blessings.
Happiness is contentment
from within.
Find a dream to follow
that will stimulate your mind.
Make laughter your partner
through life.
Be prepared to fight
for what you want or believe in.
Remember - every day is a new beginning.

You have to set realistic attainable goals that are possible to achieve.

How do you start setting goals?
Let's start with your career….
Does the type of work you do give you job satisfaction?
Are you content to be at the place where you work?
Are you spending too much time travelling to and from work?
Would you prefer working somewhere closer to home?
Are you battling to make ends meet?
Does your pay check cover your monthly expenses?
Would you like to change your job and find a new better place to work?
Ask God to guide your every step.

It's Your Time for a Mighty Breakthrough

Things might look impossible to you

but God's power is greater than you can imagine

God has no limits

God will do more for you

than you could ever ask or think

No person or obstacle can stand against God

It's not up to the world to decide on your success

It's up to God

Don't give up on your faith

Don't be discouraged

Keep believing and going forward

Keep your eyes on the prize

You don't know the wonderful things

God has waiting for you around the corner

God will bring the right people to cross your path

God will take you to a new higher level

Let God's Word repair your hurt and self-image

Make God your best friend

Praise God with your whole heart

and you will see how much God will richly reward you.

Is it your wish to have your own business?
They say the happiest people in the world are those who have made their hobby become their full time work.

Have you ever thought how you could derive sufficient income from your hobby to turn your passion into your daily work?

A lot of photographers have done this….so too have artists, models, magicians and entertainers.

If you are not happy in your job, what would be the work or career goal you would like to set for yourself?

The Sparkle of Life

Bring more joy into your life

Take time for yourself to do the things you love

Experience the joy of making something beautiful

Follow your dreams.

If your heart is longing to live life for what is true and real

If you would like to feel a deep inner fulfilment with absolute truth within

The quality of a richer life is in the stillness of your soul.

Open your heart to the sounds of nature's music

Be grateful for all the good in life

Make someone feel especially loved today

Feel the holiness of God

Connect with what is truly important in this life

Let your heart draw its strength and joy from God

Like a tiny seed it bids the response of your whole heart

to receive you, complete you and give you purpose and meaning.

Create a new life for yourself

Walk with gratitude

Become a network of love and restore your life wholly

Live in harmony with the universe
With God all things are possible
Cherish your life.

Now, let's look at your love or romantic goal.
Do you have a life partner?
Would you like to find a soul mate?
Would you like to be married?
What do you want to do for your loved one that you are not doing now?

Secrets of Life

Look for the beauty

in everything you see.

Walk in peace

showing kindness

everywhere.

The secrets of success

are motivation

and dedication

Happiness is

what you make happen

for yourself.

Caring is

going to the ends of the world

for a stranger.

Be useful with your life.

Whatever you are doing

put your whole

being into it 100%

Loving is

pleasing your loved one everyday

in a 1000 different ways.

Control your mind

you are its master

Be in control.

Live your life

without hurting or

destroying.

Believe in yourself.

Have respect for yourself.

Walk through life

always with a song.

Who do you mix with? Are they pulling you down?
Keep your goals secret or you may find your family and friends mocking you.

What are you feeding your mind every day?
Get rid of negative thinking and replacing it with positive thoughts and affirmations.
Count your blessings. Be grateful for what you've got.
What you put in, is what you get out.
As you sow, so you shall reap.

Secrets of Achieving

Your first commitment is to take responsibility for your life.

You must do what you really like doing

and what you really want to do.

Concentrate all your energy and efforts

in completing one task at a time.

Choose your main priority and plan how

you are going to achieve it.

Pray to God for guidance and direction

always giving Him thanks constantly.

You will be paid in direct proportion

to the amount of love and service you give.

Take action and make things happen now!

Be committed totally 100% to what you

want or believe in - until you get it!

The Magic in You

Keep your eyes on the stars

and the stars in your eyes

Make the most of every precious moment

Remember - every breath is a miracle

and every day is a gift

You were made with a rare uniqueness

to fulfil a special purpose

Reward yourself
with the very special things you like

Never under-estimate the power
of a seed of love
planted into another's life

Send someone a signal
that they really matter

Follow your heart's secret desires
and you will find your magic rainbow

Never give up on your dreams!

What is your spiritual goal?
After all, your life is not just a body, you have a spirit and inside a deep longing that yearns for inner peace and contentment….to be in tune with your Maker and the universe.

Would you like to get closer to God?
Is it your need and desire to love God more?
What do you want to do for God with your life?
How do you show God you need and love Him?
You could begin by making time to read and study God's Word to know God better.
And you could allocate more time to spend talking to God in prayer.

When last did you say 'thank you' to God?
Not just a quick 'thank you' but to look at your life and thank God for all the many blessings, miracles and gifts He provides you.
Thank God for every heartbeat…thank God for every breath He gives you (because your next breath is not guaranteed)…yes, thank God for your life!

YOU ARE SO PRECIOUS

If you could feel the presence of God

If you could see God's kindness
all over in every place

If you could know the strength of His power

If you could sense the depth of His love

You will begin to realize
how precious you are to God

He is always there for you
no matter what may be

God will always stand by you
loving you endlessly.

Have you ever thought about showing appreciation to God for the different parts of your body…
….like your eyes, thank God that you can see.
….your ears, thank God that you can hear.
….your hands and fingers, thank God that you can touch and feel.
…. your brain, your mind, thank God that you can think, you can dream, you can create.

….your stomach, thank God you can digest food.

….your bones, skeleton, heart, kidneys, skin, pores…there's so much to thank God for.

God Is Your Partner

All David had was just 5 stones and a sling

and God gave him the victory

All the boy had was only 5 loaves and 2 fishes

and God used this to feed 5000

All Moses could speak was with a stuttering tongue

and God chose him to free his people

God can use
whatever you may
have

When you pray with all your heart
your prayers become miracles
When you sow seeds of praise
your love for God will be greatly rewarded

When you make God your priority
your life will have deep fulfilment.

Have you made a list of your materialistic or monetary goals?
What would you like to own?
A new car?
A swimming pool?

A tennis court?
New clothing or furniture?
Are there any countries or places you would like to travel to?
What are your family goals?
What do you want to do for your parents and your children?
What are your friendship goals?
What do you want to do for your friends?
How do you stay motivated?
How do you keep on track?
You could download free inspirational and motivational books.
What should you do when you have reached and achieved one of your goals?
Go ahead and set yourself another goal in the same specific area of your life.

There's Only Jesus

If you're looking for supernatural help

with miracles and blessings

If you're looking for kindness overflowing

and the truest friend you'll ever find

If you're looking for real happiness

and the greatest love there is

There's only Jesus
Through Him, God gives all.

If you are looking for a better job, I want you to prepare and send out 30 emails (one email every day)…it's so easy to do…all you have to do is copy and paste the exact same email to 30 different owners of companies where you would like to work telling them what you would like to do for them….tell them how you could contribute and what you would like to do in the company.

Finding a job is really a numbers game. The more emails you send out, the greater your chance will be of succeeding.

Would you love to learn to play a musical instrument?...
or would you like to learn to speak a new language?

Become who you want to be.
Be true to yourself.
Follow your heart
to the path of greatness that lies within you.
Focus your time and energy on your daily priorities.
Put God's Word first and there will be wonderful victories ahead.

Find a way to serve others and you will
be fulfilled.
Thank God for all His blessings you are
receiving today.
Look for ways to create happiness for
yourself
and for your loved ones.
Protect your heart with all diligence,
for out of it flow the issues of life.
Make God your first choice when you
call for help.
Dream big dreams.

You Hold the Key

Let your determination

be so strong that nothing

can sway its course.

Let your mind believe

so intensely that your dreams

become reality.
Let your actions be rich
with enthusiasm that it moves
the hearts of all.

Let your life be filled
with greater purpose
To reach Higher
To think bigger
To love deeper
than you've ever done before!

Our lives are shaped by the goals that we set and strive for.
Meaningful goals are the prerequisite for all
achievements.
Author unknown

No person has successfully fulfilled God's
dream for his life
until he positively affects the lives of others.
Dr John Maxwell

Secrets of Living

Don't look at how big your problem is ....look at how big God is.

A big secret of life is

to always

have something

to look forward to tomorrow.

Love is kindness - loving is giving with all your heart.

Saturate yourself with the Word of God

and you will have wonderful victories.

Make time everyday

to separate yourself away from the world

to love God.

Be committed to your major goal

with singleness of purpose.

Feed your mind daily

with good positive healthy energy.

Always have a dream

to excite you

and make plans on how

you are going to achieve it.

Be a blessing to people

by contributing and making a difference to the world around you.

God Cares Deeply About You

Whatever trouble you might be facing in your life

Whatever storm clouds are on the horizon

Whatever roadblocks are standing in your way

God cares deeply about you.

If you're looking for true victory in your life

then give your love to Jesus

Faster than lightening can strike

**and quicker than a wheel can turn
God will move in a miraculous way
to create wonderful miracles for you!**

What are your priorities in your life?
What is absolutely vital and a must-have necessity in your life?
You've got to separate your needs from your greeds.
Remember, a journey of a hundred miles begins with only one step.

Start working today toward your goals.
Begin immediately and take that first step.
List the steps you need to take, and what you need to do to move forward.

Dear Friend

I just had to write this to you….

I've just got to tell you something important….

I know things for you haven't been easy…you've been through a lot….you've been deeply hurt….your pain is intense ….you've been wondering why your life has been through so much trouble….so much frustration…so many tests, trials and hardship.

You've been let down ….you've been disappointed time and time again….you've given up hope and just don't care any more….

I just want to tell you that in all this….God is here.

God has seen every tear that you have cried….God has felt your pain and knows what you are going through…God really wants to help you ….He is there….but you have to first turn the key….you have to open the door wide.

When a heart is broken….when a life is in ruin….it's not easy to pick up the pieces and start all over again….but you have to!....there's no other way up!....you have to let go!....it's a brand new season….it's the start of a new day….I know you just can't forget what has happened…… but you have to make a new life for yourself….you have to get out of the river and walk over to the mountain….there is help ….and there is hope.

The Hand of God

Things are now going to change for you….life is going to start getting better….you're now on your way to a new beginning….tell me, what do you want out of life?....what are your deepest dreams that you want to see come true?.....what is very important to you?.....what do you value the most?

Life isn't just a straight line….it's got curves, bends, ups and downs….you've had a lot of down-time for too long now…..it's now time for you to rise up….you know all the beauty that once was in your heart….it can still be found if you search deep within….you know what's true and you know your feelings…the dreams and wishes you have that you want to see come true….but how is this all going to happen for you?....how do you make a lemon into a lemonade?....how do you find the way to a more richer fulfilment?

THE POWER OF ALMIGHTY GOD

Please don't look to man for the answers….you will be

disappointed….please don't try to find the solution all by yourself….our ways are so limited and we are very fragile and weak….but there is a God who is here with almighty power, and all the know-how in the world, together with all the ability, divine intervention and strength to change each and everything in your life all for the better.

If God could make water come out of a rock for Moses….then it's easy for God to make a miracle in your life all in an instant. If God could create a man out of just dust….then surely God can bring about exciting wonderful changes in your life.

You are a child of God

What do you have to do to see your miracle take place?

What should you do to start a new life?....to make things better?.... to bring blessings, gifts and wonders come your way? All you've got to do is ask God?....but maybe you already have done this and nothing has happened....why did your requests not come to pass?....did you ask God for greed or for need?

The wisdom of Solomon

Let's look at King Solomon… what did he ask God for?.....he didn't ask for things of this world like a mansion, palace or castle filled with lots of gold and treasure …..all Solomon asked God for was for wisdom …..but God looked at his heart and saw that his heart was pure….God gave him knowledge and wisdom together with understanding ….because Solomon didn't look for self-gain and did not ask for worldly greed but Solomon asked for spiritual blessings and needs….God was so moved by Solomon's request that God gave him wisdom plus on top of that, God enriched his life with treasure in such great abundance!

The Greatest Power in the World

When you come to God you are coming to a King….not just any King….but the King of the Universe, Creator of everything. Yes, God is your Father and you are His beloved child, but God is holy, upright and pure…God is so beautiful ….our minds just cannot conceive, think or imagine how magnificent, how glorious, how amazing and how brilliant is our God….there are no words which we know that can describe God's loveliness, His awesomeness, His splendour!

Before you look at your needs and all the things that you want from God…..let's look at what God wants from us.

What is God looking for? What pleases God?....God wants recognition…God wants acceptance….God wants our appreciation….God wants our love….God wants a relationship with us....God wants us to get to know Him….but How?

By reading and studying God's Word we find out what God likes…. Tell God you love Him…let God know that there is nothing in your life more vital, more necessary or more important than Him!

Even the little things

Don't take God for granted…thank God for even the little things….did you ever say thank you to God for water?....where would we be without water? …..thank God for the streams, rivers, waterfalls, the oceans, the springs and the rain ….how about saying thank you to God for sand?....that's right, I'm being serious, without the soil, the earth….without the ground ….we won't have food….there would not be vegetables or fruit ….nor flowers, nor trees and grass!

Don't come to God every day with the same boring prayer!....get yourself a book and write down the things that you need to say 'thank you' to God for….you've got to move God's heart….you've got to touch God by showing Him that you are grateful for even the tiny little things in your life.

Thank God for the gift of air….for the breath of life….thank God that He has given mankind the ability to think and create inventions to make our lives easier and more enjoyable…inventions like the fridge, the computer, electricity. God just doesn't want lip service....you must truly believe and feel it in your heart for what you are thanking Him for.

Don't be lazy and just say 'thank you God for everything'…..No! You must be specific!....you must tell God which blessings, gifts or miracles you are grateful for.

Why is it so important to say thank you to God?

Imagine that you are a child and on Monday you come to your father and ask him for money for clothing….without hesitation, he gives this to you….then on Tuesday, you come again and ask for more money to go out and have a good time with your friends….and again he lovingly gives this to you….and a few days later, you ask your father again for something that you want….How does your father feel? ….every time you ask for something, but he never hears you say 'thank you'….your father begins to feel that you are always demanding more and more without showing appreciation.

It's the same with God…He is our Father and we are His children….God is not a shopping mall or a money bank….you can't just come to Him and expect Him to give you what you want without ever thanking Him for all the many, exceptional and wonderful gifts and blessings He has already given you….Thank you God that I can walk, stand, sit….thank you God for sleep, for rest, for peace…Thank you God for the beautiful gift of colours….for the stars….for the seasons….for the gift of music…for all the different types and varieties of flowers….for herbs and vitamins….Thank you Father God for Jesus….

Every day, take time to thank God for different specific gifts and blessings in your life …..for things that you have never thanked Him for before.

Start a 'I'm grateful for list'…. Look at all the amazing wonders of nature….marvel at the miracle of your brain….the precious gift of your eyes….your living skin.

Your life will have a deep inner fulfilment and take on a new meaning….you will realize that God is truly good and God wants to bless you more and more….and when you show God that you do not take Him for granted and all that He has already given you….all that He has already done….like all the times He has protected you….and for all the days He has loved you ….for His patience…for His forgiveness and grace….

When you show God that you are grateful even for the small things in your life….when your heart is filled with appreciation and praise, you will always be rewarded with mighty miracles.

You have the power of choice and the gift of prayer to change the circumstances and situations in your life….when God looks at your heart, will He see gratitude?

SHOW YOUR LOVE TO GOD

SENT BY GOD

I was in a supermarket pushing a trolley, doing my weekly grocery shopping when suddenly a woman, dressed in a long black dress, came up behind me and began shouting at me:
'Why have you stopped praising God?'
I ignored her and just kept on walking, looking at my grocery list what to buy next.

'Hey you! I'm talking to you! Why have you stopped praising God?'

She would not leave me alone and kept on following me and carried on repeating 'Why have you stopped praising God?'

I was angry. 'Listen here…you don't know me…you are a total stranger to me…you don't know what I do…how can you say that I have stopped praising God?'

She answered: 'I've been sent by God to give you a message…

Do you know why you are out of work, why you don't have a job and things are not going well for you?

The reason your life is a mess is that you have stopped praising God!

And because of this, you see the angels of God have now stopped working for you.

I want you to get back, my friend and continue praising God with all your heart and you will see the messengers of God will be helping and working for you.'

The stranger in black dress with long sleeves walked away and disappeared in the crowd of shoppers.

I thought about what she had said…

Yes, it was all true what she had said…I had to do something about the way my life was going.
I listened and followed her advice …and things started changing for the better with huge unexplained miracles happening, as I began to thank and offer God praise.

Trust in the Lord with all your heart and lean not on your own understanding.
but in all your ways acknowledge Him, and He will direct your path.
Proverbs 3:5,6

Eye hath not seen
nor ear heard
neither have entered into the heart of man
the things which God hath prepared for them that love him.

1 Corinthians 2:9

Count Your Blessings

Count your blessings instead of your crosses

Count your gains instead of your losses

Count your joys instead of your woes

Count your friends instead of your foes

Count your smiles instead of your tears

Count your courage instead of your fears

Count your full years instead of your lean

Count your kind deeds instead of your mean

Count your health instead of your wealth

Count on God instead of yourself.

PRAYER

There is no greater joy

than loving God in prayer

There are no riches more rewarding

than the eternal treasures you'll receive

Prayer brings powerful help into your life

Prayer changes circumstances

What a wonderful privilege we have

to give our heart to our Father in prayer.

How to get paid appearing in TV Ads and Soapies

By Bernard Levine

Have you ever wished you could get a job appearing in TV Advertisements? .... like the Samsung or Nokia cell phone ads, McDonald's or Coca Cola ads.
Would you like to be in a TV soapie or serial?
Now's your chance to make your dreams come true.
It's so much fun and the money you will earn will be well worth it!

Happiness is what you make happen for yourself.

Okay, let's get started. Producers of TV Ads and serials are always on the look out for new faces, new talent to appear in their stories or advertisements.
It does not matter if you have no teeth or if you only have one

eye....they can still use you and want you to be in their list of cast members.

In fact, very often, the producers are not looking for attractive pretty faces...they would rather prefer someone who looks a little different...someone who stands out in the crowd ...even if you have a crooked nose or you are short and plump....it doesn't matter what you look like...they still need you to be in their soapies or advertisements.

They are always looking for a variety and a host of different characters...they are looking for new faces and new identities....so the prettiest girl in the block doesn't always get the job.

You need an employment agency which is called a 'Casting Agency' to get you work on TV.

If you don't know any names of Casting Agencies' look them up on Google.

Do a search for Casting Agents in your area close to where you live.

Here are the names of some of the biggest and most popular Casting Agencies in America: (look up their addresses and contact numbers)

Creative Artists Agency (CAA)
United Talent Agency (UTA)
William Morris Endeavor Entertainment (WME)
International Creative Management (ICM)
Osbrink Talent Agency
Paradigm Talent Agency
www.starnow.com

Search on Google for the names and contact numbers of

the top British Casting Agencies.

You'll find that there are so many casting agencies for you to choose from.
Phone them up and tell them you want to be on TV.
Ask them about the days and times they are open and if you need to make an appointment, or when would be the best time for you to go in and see them.
Also ask them if there is a joining fee.
If there is an enrolment fee, rather find an agent who will not charge you to sign up.

When you arrive at the Casting Agency, they will give you a form to complete so that they will have your information on file to contact you for all the jobs that come up, and of course they need your bank details so that they can pay you.

Once you have completed the application form with all your personal information like your name, address, contact numbers, the colour of your eyes and hair...your height (they very often ask you to stand against the wall so they can measure you)...sometimes they want to know whether you can ride a horse, or swim, speak any foreign languages just in case any of these roles come up.

Next, the casting agency needs to create your portfolio of head-and-shoulders photos showing a variety of different moods such as how you look when you are smiling, sad or angry.

They will ask you to stand against the wall or against a back-drop and start clicking away.

You should not have to pay for the photos that they take of you.

There will be head and shoulder photos, left front profile, right front profile, back profile, side profile and full body profile, standing and sitting.

The casting agency will choose and send the very best of your photos to producers including their contacts at advertising companies who are looking for new TV talent.

When the TV Producers find a character that they like and want to feature in their soapie or advertisement, they will contact your Casting Agency to ask for you by name.

Now the exciting part begins. You receive a phone call from your Casting Agency to tell you that you have been selected to appear in XYZ Soap or a McDonalds TV advertisement. Your Casting Agency will ask you if you will be available for the shoot to take place on..... at such and such place. They will let you know what your payment will be and if you agree, they will ask you to go to a wardrobe dressing so they can fit you with the clothes they want you to wear on the day they film.

They will tell you where the dress fitting will be taking place and the time you should be there.

Sometimes, they will email you a script of a few words you will have to learn which you are going to say in the program or ad.

At the Wardrobe, you will be meeting and seeing other characters who will also have a role to play in your program or ad.

The Casting Agency, together with the Producer decide on the look or type of character they want you to portray. They will select the different items of clothing which they want you to go and try on at the wardrobe fitting.

After trying on several suits of clothing for the Producer to see, they will choose the clothing they like and want you to wear.

If there are any alterations to be done, they will take measurements and the items will be given to the dressmaker or tailor.

Then comes the big day of the shoot.

You arrive on time at the venue where the filming is about to take place.

Your clothing will be ready, clean, altered and pressed for you to get dressed in.

Then, once you are dressed, you will need to go to the Make-up department to comb and style your hair and colour your face all ready for the shoot.

In the meanwhile, you will be waiting your turn while others are being filmed.

The Producers will make sure that they are happy and satisfied with your scene. Most often, they will ask you to shoot your role over again several times so that they can choose which 'take' they like the best.

You will then go to lunch, together with all the cast members and crew and could even find yourself sitting next to the main Stars of the show! After the shoot is over, you leave the venue and go on your way home with lots of news to tell your family and friends about what you did and how it all happened.

The next day, you should call your Casting Agency to find out when you could expect to receive payment for the filming.

There are different ways you could be paid.

Sometimes, you will receive an agreed flat rate... a fixed amount for the filming...but in other instances, you will be paid every time your ad is shown and aired on TV....and then again, in months or even years to come, if your ad is repeated, you will again receive payment for your role that you originally did way back then! The rate of payment is usually much higher for ads, then when you are filming a soapie.

The reason is that soapies are not usually sponsored, while Advertisers and companies pay big money to have their names, products or services featured on TV.
Think how much money Coca Cola's TV budget is for advertising ...and what about

BMW or Mercedes Benz! They spend a fortune and are willing to pay handsomely to get their message broadcast across the world.

Then, later in the week, the phone will ring again.
'Hello, it's your Casting Agency.'
Why are they calling you?
'Hello, we have another shoot for you to do....this time it's for Colgate toothpaste.
The shoot will take place in a restaurant and you will be filmed while having coffee and

cake...all you have to do is pretend that you are talking on your cell phone and....
Will you be available on Sunday at 10am to be at Bella Napoli restaurant in LA?'

Going for TV Auditions

As part of your experience in the TV world, your phone will ring and you will get a call from your Casting Agent to invite you to go for an audition. They will give you the name of the product or the TV series that you have been chosen for,

including the time and place of the audition, and the role they want you to audition for.
They will also let you know how much money you will be paid and if there are any lines they want you to say.
They will email you the script so you can practise your lines before the audition.

You arrive at the audition, waiting your turn and when they call your number you stand in front of the camera and they tell you what they want you to do.

In a few days time, the Casting Agent will call you to tell you if you got the job.

If you got the role, they will ask you to go for a wardrobe fitting so that you can try on the clothes they need you to wear on the day that you are filming.

You can get paid doing Voice Overs

To find voice over jobs, you need to have a Voice Over Agent and you should register samples of your voice at a Voice Bank.

For Voice Over jobs have a look at:

https://www.upwork.com/o/jobs/browse/skill/voice-over/

www.intervoiceover.com

Search on Google for Voice Over Agents in the area that you live.

If you can do various accents, let them hear your talent.

You can get paid as a Narrator

You'll have lots of fun and be well paid when you join ACX. www.acx.com

You can get paid as a Translator

If you know how to converse in another language (or more),

you can make money being a Translator.
Have a look at:
www.babelcube.com

You can get paid for your photo in Magazines and Product Catalogs

You should ask if your Casting Agents can get your photos to be featured in product catalogs, or on street billboards including magazine and newspaper advertisements.
This will be another wonderful great source of income for you.

If you still want to get more additional work, you could list your name together with your profile and your photo in the entertainment industry's Contacts Directory published by Spotlight.

To be on TV is a great way to make money, meet new people and have lots of fun....and it's exciting to have your family and friends see you and your children appearing on TV and your photo published in magazines.

You are definitely going to have lots of fun!

100's of Opportunities for you
to make money

By Bernard Levine

This unique book will show you hundreds of different ways you can make money.

If you would like to receive an extra second income….

If you want to have more money coming into your bank account every month….

Then this book is a life-saver.

There are so many ways that you can make money in your spare time doing what you are good at and doing what you love. There is something here for everybody!

Many of these legitimate income opportunities will put cash into your wallet or purse, without you stepping outside of your home.

For you to have a regular flow of money coming into your life, you need to have the know-how and wisdom of what you need to do to make it happen for you.

You need to know the names of the companies that will pay you.

You need to have several streams of income and sources of continuous cash being deposited into your bank account.

And there's more than just one way to make money.

The secret of success is what you make happen for yourself.

You are only a few minutes away, to get started and be on the road to getting dollars paid regularly into your bank account.

So, what are you waiting for....

This unique book will show you hundreds of different ways and ideas how you will have a continuous flow of extra income coming into your life!
Choose the opportunities you like the best and let your income begin!

Why I wrote this book?

I want to help you make money.

I want you to have a constant flow of income pouring into your life.

I don't want you to be limited by the salary that your daily job gives you….

Or perhaps you don't even have a job or a monthly income….

In this unique book, I have listed lots and lots of various ways that you will be able to make money….part time or full time.

You will be able to choose what you would like to do and in each category of income providers there are lists of companies who will accept you and pay you and continue to pay you.

Contents

Things you can do that will bring in a second income

Get paid for your digital photos

Companies who will print and sell your photos on products

List of where to sell your artwork

Directories of Freelance Writing Jobs

Make money selling all kinds of things

Become a published author

Make money with your voice

Companies that pay you to teach online

Sell your recipes

Sell your jokes

Be a star on TV

Get paid for your words published in newspapers and magazines

Create and sell royalty free music

How to turn your trash into money

Plus lots of lists of hundreds of wonderful opportunities for you to end that 9 to 5 job and start your own business as well as many other ideas and ways that will bring you cash and change your life!

Let's start off with a list of

some things you can do to bring in a second income:

Antique and Collectibles Dealer

Book and Magazine Dealer

Apartment Locator

Debt Collection Agency

Computer Tutor for Children

Online copywriter

Correspondence Club

Dating and Escort Service

Directory Publisher

Employment Agency

Errand Service

Flea Market Seller

Gift Basket Business

Magic at children's birthday parties

Food Delivery Service

Freelance Photographer

Freelance Writer

Make your own greeting cards and sell them

Image and Influence Consultant

Babysitting and daycare

Baking/cooking

Start an online shop

Give music lessons

Photography lessons Web programming Computer repair Social Media consulting

Cooking or baking lessons to moms and their children

Fitness instruction

Nutrition consultations

Write Slogans for Major Companies Life coaching

Style consultations

Beauty consultations

Gardening help

Clean homes

Invitation Printing

Matchmaker Service

Make merit and award

certificates

Newsletter Publishing

Newspaper Clipping Service

Personalized Stationery

Photography family portraits, animals, children, events Portrait and Wedding Photography

Make custom wooden furniture

Pet sitting

Advertising Manager

Bookkeeping

Reflexologist

Yoga

Facilitat

or

Teach

dance

classes

Hula hoop maker

Make and sell baby headbands and blankets Make and sell handmade jewellery

Printing Broker

Metal Detecting ….Buy a second hand metal detector and search for treasure.

Printer Toner Recharging

Printing Invitations

Proof-reader

Kid's Party Entertainer

Real Estate Magazine

Real Estate Agent

Sell bottled water at events

Reporter

Restaurant Delivery Service

Rubber Stamps

School Photographer especially at their sport events Be a voice over artist

Apartment Preparation Service

Telemarketing

Using Your Car or Van to Make Money Sell flower arrangements

Start an office cleaning company

Garden maintenance

Home cleaning

Make your own sauces and sell at flea markets Make and sell birdhouses and bird feeders Make scratch boards and tunnels for cats

Last minute accommodation

Writing Press Releases

Start a list of Properties to rent in your area Start an area newspaper and sell advertising

Sell plastic, cardboard, newspapers, metal, bottles, cans

Sell celebrity autographed photos (which you get for free) to restaurants and interior decorators…

See 'Make Money collecting first edition books, get free celebrity autographs and more by Bernard Levine'.

Baby Sitting service

Make your own bottled pickles and cultured foods to sell List of holiday homes to rent

Put poetry
onto trays,
mirrors Print
or make and
sell car-signs

Taxi Service for seniors, children and everyone Public Speaking

Sell car
manuals
Sell
second
hand toys

Sell sheet music manuscripts

Paint and sell pine cones as Christmas decorations

Find sterling silver at charity shops to sell on Ebay

Look for vintage watches to sell

Sell porcelain

Vinyl Records   Sell on Ebay

Sell corporate gifts

Health consulting

Virtual Assisting

Be a presenter

Make money collecting and selling

See '**Make money collecting everyday easy to find items**

By Bernard Levine'   ISBN-13: 978-1503172036

Did you know you can get paid for your digital photos?

Have a look at these websites to see how it all works:

iStock Photo

SmugMug

Alamy

Flickr Collection

Fotolia

Dreamstime

Photoshelter

Shutterstock

123RF They are looking for new photos to license Can Stock Photo

Camera Dollars

Foap   Recommended

Clashot   Take pics and

make money Sell your photos on eBay

Companies who will print and sell your photos on products

Cafepress   Give them any photo and they will sell your photos printed on coffee mugs, T-shirts, aprons, mouse-pads, plus a huge range of many other exciting gifts.

Zazzle   They print your digital photos onto cell phone covers, fridge magnets, wall hangings and even onto a teddy bear's bib! They have so many wonderful gifts products for you to choose. They will advertise and sell your photos printed on their gift items for you.

Pixels   They put your photo's on T-shirts.

Companies who will sell

your artwork

Fine Art America They will sell your paintings, drawings, prints and photographs to dealers and interior decorators all over the world.

ArtPal sells your paintings, prints, photography, sculptures, handmade jewellery, and crafts online.

DeviantArt

Directories of Freelance Writing Jobs

If you are looking for regular freelance writing jobs, then you should list your name on any one or all of these sites:

Elance   Very popular job portal of unlimited opportunities Guru   There are hundreds of writing projects available Demand Studios

Write Jobs   See their job listings

TutToaster

EHow

editfast.com   Jobs for proofreaders, writers, copy editors

Break Studios

WritersCafe.org   Write on any subject you like Pro Blogger They have lots of job listings

The Dabbling Mum   Writers with expertise in direct sales
Fundsforwriters.com   Lists paying writing markets

Newsvine

Constant Content

DailyArticle

Upwork   Lots of writing opportunities

WorldwideFreelance.com

Listverse.com

MediaBistro   Copywriting jobs

Freelancer

Workersonboard.com

Textbroker   Earn money online writing content

Wise Geek   Get paid to write articles

Lovetoknow

Make money selling all kinds of things

If you have any unwanted items that you

want to sell for cash, list your items on any of the following popular websites:

Ebay

Bid or Buy

Tradesy   No cost to list your items

Thredup   They pay you upfront for the items you want to sell

Amazon

Shopify

Poshmark

Idonowldont

Decluttr   Sell your CDs, DVDs, and video games

Clickbank   Sell ebooks

Takealot.com

SchoolsTrader

Appliances Instruction manuals   Sell these

on Ebay

Gift Card Rescue   Sell your gift cards and get cash for them

Make money with your voice

Get paid and make money recording authors books as a narrator.

ACX.com

Teach English and other lessons online and earn a second income:

Udemy Teach online and share your knowledge

Italki

VerbalPlanet

TutorABC

Samespeak

Verbling

Tutor.com

Rosetta Stone Studio Online language coaching

AceYourCollegeClasses.com

TeachStreet

SkillShare

Wyzant   Earn big money

TutorTree

Sell your recipes

Companies who will publish your very own paperback recipe book:

Payloadz.com   A paid service to sell downloadable items

Sell jokes

Publish and sell your jokes in a Joke eBook.

Reader's Digest   They pay when your jokes are published

Be a star on TV

You could become an extra or actor….no experience needed…they are always looking for new faces and new talent:

Starnow

Be On Screen

2020 casting

Uni-versal EXTRAS

Casting Collective

Get paid for your words published in newspapers and magazines

http://allindiewriters.com/writers-markets/

Sell poetry and verse

Hallmark

Cappers – $10 per poem

Standard Publishing – Pays $25 per poem

Blue Mountain Arts Pays $300

Pockets $25 and more for poetry

Good Old Days $15 per poem

Alive Now! $35 and more

Oatmeal Studios Pays $75 per card

Moonlighting Cards Pays $25 per slogan Gallant Greeting Corp

American Greetings

Ephemera, Inc   Pays $50 per slogan

Kalan

Rockshots

Snafu Designs   Pays $100 per slogan/idea

Love Greeting Cards, Inc   They pay $100 to $300

Get paid for writing

www.4writers.net

www.Academia-research.com   Highest salaries

www.essaywriters.net

www.myessays.com

http://www.joomlajumpstart.com/paid-writing

Words of Worth

http://www.articleincome.com/howitworks.html

Freelancewritinggigs.com

https://www.ibpublishing.com/   Very

good!

Freelancewritingcenter.com   High compensation

Constant Content pays you twice a week

eCopywriters   Pays twice a month

Clickworker.com   Recommended

Get paid to review websites

DooYoo

Ciao.co.uk

Reviewstream.com   Write product reviews and get paid Epinions

Shvoong.com

Sharedreviews.com

Rateitall.com

Softwarejudge.com   Paid for your opinions

Usertesting.com   Get paid to test

Payperpost

SocialSpark

LoudLaunch

SponsoredReviews

BuyBlogReviews

Create and sell royalty free music

ProductionTrax.com

Create something useful to sell on Etsy

Knitting

Embroidery

Cross stitch

Decoupage

Jewellery making

Painting

Scrapbooking

Sculpting

Drawing

Crocheting

Wreath making

Quilting

Pottery

Papermache

Beading

Sewing   Make clothes, bags, scatter cushions

Woodworking

Calligraphy   Do certificates, wedding and party invitations

Candle Making   Make your own shapes and scents

Cake Decorating

Graphic Design   Get free software programs online

Buy second hand furniture at charity shops and sandpaper, paint or reupholster for a great resale price.

Sell Things You Find Outside

Branches to a local florist

Pinecones make beautiful holiday decorations

Driftwood

Sea shells

Pressed wildflowers

Dried vines

Sell CDs and/or DVDs

Put your music collection on a computer or external hard drive, then sell the original discs on Ebay.

Decluttr   Sell your CDs, DVDs, and video games

Musicmagpie

There's Cash In Your Trash

Bottles and Cans   Sell to

Schupan Recycling Scrap Metal

www.simsmm.com/sell-to-us

Copper Sell to American Scrap Co.

InkjetCartridge.com They buy your empty cartridges TonerBuyer.com   Sell them your old cartridges WeBuySupplies.com They buy toner and ink cartridges Moving BoxesBoxQuest.com

Yemm & Hart Green Materials buys corks for recycling.

TerraCycle will pay you for your trash

Sell baby clothing, furniture, toys

Just Between Friends

StorkBrokers

Sell your Books

Cash 4 Books   Sell used books and text books

Abebooks.com   Highly recommended

Sellitback.com

Fatbrain.co.uk

Half.com

Good Reads   Sell your eBooks

Bookscouter   You can compare prices and sell your books for the highest price

Sell Second hand clothing

Kindermint

ThredUp

Poshmark

Sell Electronics

Gazelle buys old smart phones, tablets, laptops, and PC's.

Sell Tickets

StubHub Sell your concert or sport tickets to the world's largest ticket marketplace.

Direct Marketing Companies

Avon

Mary Kay

Amway

Herbalife

Tupperware

Scentsy

Buy and sell domain names

Sedo.com

GoDaddy Auctions

Flippa

Where to find things you can resell

Flea markets

Charity stores

Yard sales

Salvage

Clearance sales

eBay

Craiglist

Sell your crafts, knitting, handmade jewellery

Cargoh

Etsy

Craft Foxes

Get paid for your design

99Designs.com

Threadless

Get paid to do random jobs

TaskRabbit

Zaarly

Be a driver

Lyft

Uber

Find photography jobs

Thumbtack

Make money playing music at weddings and events

Gigmasters

Gigsalad

WeddingWire

Get paid to deliver

Postmates

Promote products on the street

Street Team Promotion

Get paid for your opinion

Focus Pointe Global

Toluna

SwagBucks

MySurvey.com

Opinion Outpost

iPoll

Hiving

Be a Telemarketer

Intrep.com

Make money writing slogans

Slogan Slingers

Get a Slogan

Sell home and health products

Jamberry Nails

Thirty-One Gifts

Mary & Martha

Zeal for Life

Juice Plus

Nerium International

Premier Designs

Younique

Norwex

WildTree

Radiantly You

Plexus Slim

Nikken

DoTerra

Young Living Essential Oils

HOW TO FIND A JOB QUICKLY AND EASILY
By Bernard Levine

Let me start off by saying, that I know that this book is going to be highly controversial and people will be shocked by the methods and techniques which I provide to help and enable someone to get a job.

Because the ways spoken about in this unique book are not the everyday norm (how the mass and every Tom, Dick and Harry goes about getting a job) ….your first response will probably be that the ideas expressed in this book are wrong and will not work…but before you attack, criticise and condemn, hold onto your horses! I'm telling you, that although the ways will all seem strange and perhaps even bizarre, never mind, I am not writing this book to please the Employment Personnel Agencies, and this book is not going to appeal to the staff who are working in Human Resources in gigantic Corporations…this book is aimed at the unemployed who are sick and tired of being rejected time and time again…having their CV's thrown into File 13 without ever getting

any feedback, response to their job applications leaving them angry, frustrated and depressed.
But that's exactly why it does work because instead of you doing what everybody else does and standing in a long row trying to get them to notice and accept you….this book will show you how you are going to stand out from the rest…how you will make a big impression and how your interview and you yourself will be well remembered.

So, we are going to try something different ….we are going on a very different route to find and secure a job. I'm not interested in what others who are smug in their well paid jobs have to say, nor do I care.
I'm going to go out of my way to give people hope, using a little imagination and igniting the sparks of greatness that lead to a path of success and victory.

Thinking of You

I am thinking of you today

and I want you to know

that no matter what your situation is

God's help is so mighty

Keep your eyes on His awesome power

and your heart focused on His never-ending love

Ask God to open the door that is closed

to make the way clear for you

His strength is beyond our understanding

His ways are so miraculous and complete

God deeply loves you

And your victory is just around the corner!

Dear Reader
I want you to know, that I am passionate and determined to see that you get a job and find it quickly and urgently!

And for you to find a job, you must always remember...
getting a job is just a numbers game...that's what it is!
I repeat, and cannot stress enough that the way you are going to find a job will be a numbers game.
Let me explain and illustrate what I mean and how it really will be by telling you a true story.
This tale I am about to tell you, is the working principle of how getting a job really is and has become.

With our huge population, there are lots of mice out there that are all chasing the same block of cheese.

Because the availability of these jobs are sometimes very limited, with so many candidates all applying for the same job, the secret is you have to stand out from the pack and be head and shoulders way above the rest.

This story might shock you, but that is part of my plan. You see the reason I am going to tell you this story, is that I want the message of the story to stick and stay in your mind…I want you to know that the truth you will discover in this story, will be like finding a job.

Here is what really happened….

You see, there is this guy, let's call him Abe….he wakes up in the morning with a dreadful unbearable pain inside.

Abe goes to the Doctor who examines him and tells him: 'Abe, it breaks my heart to tell you this news….

Abe, you have an incurable disease and only have 3 days on average to live. I'm sorry I can't help you. You've lived a fairly long life…how old are you now?'

Abe answered: 'I'm 88'.

The Doctor responded: 'Is there anything that you regret in your life that you were not able to do? …or shall I say, that you wanted to do, but never got around to doing it?'

Abe replied: 'Yes, Doctor there is this one thing….

I've never kissed a woman?'

The Doctor's face showed his surprise: 'How come you have never been able to do this?'

Abe added: 'You see Doctor…I'm very short, I have pimples on my face and as you know, I stutter ...

and because of all this, women find me very unattractive!'

The Doctor smiled and said: 'Abe, I know a way that you will definitely have your wish come true….here's how you will get the success you are looking for….

All you've got to do is on a Saturday morning, go visit a busy Shopping Mall, go early…be there just before the shops open and stand outside a busy store and every woman you see that passes by, you say to her:

'Hi, my name is Abe…I want to kiss you!' Even if she is holding a man's hand, it doesn't matter, you just carry on telling every woman that you see 'My name is Abe…I want to kiss you! What have you got to lose?'

Abe could hardly believe his ears what his trusted Doctor had just told him…Abe wanted to be absolutely sure and asked: 'Will it work Doctor?'

The Doctor answered: 'The law of averages will never let you down! It's a numbers game. All of your 88 years you have not succeeded in knowing how it feels to kiss a woman…now I'm telling you, if you want to see results this will definitely work…it's a guaranteed method!   Take it from me and just go do what I told you to do....If you don't try, you will never know! It's Saturday tomorrow, so why don't you choose a busy Shopping Centre, be positive and the results will come!'

So Abe went along to Sandon Shopping Mall and he stood outside Woolworths. The first woman strolled past…

'Hi! My name is Abe. I want to kiss you?'

'X@y&*z,' You Pig!!! she walked away totally disgusted.

The second woman that Abe saw and approached, spat in his face.

The third woman's response was to hit him in the eye!

But the Doctor told Abe not to stop but to just carry on regardless.

At 5 o'clock, the Doctor arrived at the Shopping Mall to see how Abe was getting on.

'Look at me Doctor! I have a black eye, I have been sworn at, kicked and spat upon! Your method doesn't work!'

The Doctor was astonished and taken aback: 'I'm really terribly sorry Abe…I can't understand why it did not work…I mean how many women did you ask? How many women walked past?'

'There was at least a hundred that walked by that I approached and asked' Abe sadly replied.

 'Well Abe! It should have worked! I tell you what, you must be very hungry….sit down and relax while I go get you a cheese burger, some chips and a coke…I won't be long!'.

After fifteen minutes, the Doctor returned with the food and drink but Abe was no where to be found.

The Doctor then phoned Abe 'I've got the food…where are you? '

Abe laughed 'You see Doctor, I decided to just carry on talking to the ladies….and when you left, this woman walks past and I called out 'My name is Abe…I want to kiss you!'

She replied: 'Yes, certainly! I would like to kiss you too! Shall we go to your place or mine?'

'I'm now at her home and we are getting to know each other!'

If you think about it, the principle, the success and the results of finding a job are exactly the same as this story.

How can you expect to find a job if you only approach one company? You might be lucky, but I'm not talking about luck! I'm talking about maximizing your chances and increasing the possibilities of actually securing a job offer.

The more companies you try, the more opportunities and chances of success you will have.

Here's what I want you to do....

Get hold of your local area Yellow Pages (or find the 'Yellow Pages' on the web or at your nearest library)

Start going through the Yellow Pages phone book looking at the many different categories where businesses, companies and services are advertised…. for example… you will find...Accounting Software, Stationery Manufacturers, Motor Vehicle Spares, Fibreglass Moulding, Pharmaceutical Companies….and so on.

Make a list of the companies where you would like to work, taking note of the physical address where they are situated. How far would you have to travel to get to work?

If possible, you don't want to have to travel too far to get to and from work every day…so choose wisely companies situated in areas close to your home.

Now, get a notepad and pen and write down your list of at least 20 companies in areas close to your home, where you would like to work.

Next, make a list of all the different kinds of jobs that you are able to do….or the specific jobs that you would like to do at the companies which you have just listed.

Remember, that if you only put down one type of work that you are willing to perform or do at a company, then you are cutting short and limiting your chances of success.

Here's what I mean….

If you only look for Business Analyst jobs, what will you do if there are only 6 companies where you can apply to be a Business Analyst and they all turn you down? Then you have nothing and you are back to square one!

You have to have a second or third choice of the type of work that you are able to perform at a company. You have to have a backup plan.

So, on the first page of your notebook make a list of <u>ALL</u> the various and different type of jobs you have the knowledge of and can actually do at any given company.

Here's an example….

If you want to get into sales, but the company offered you a job in telemarketing would you accept?

So now, instead of having just one position you can apply for….you have now got two different posts you can apply for instead of just one…you are creating more opportunities for yourself either being a Sales Consultant or you can also be a Telemarketer.

Would you be able to do demonstrations of products for the company?...then they could offer you a job doing promotions and demonstrations, perhaps even arranging events, sales meetings, business networking and functions, sending out invitations to buyers and clients, following up and co-ordinating the whole launch and its activities.

Could you do cold calling, like gathering information and doing research, providing leads and making sales appointments for the Consultants?

If you are able to do this, then you could become a Canvasser, a New Business Manager or work in Marketing.

Are you able to handle queries from the public, listen to their complements or complaints? …there could be good opportunities waiting for you being in Customer Care or Reception.

I want you to prepare and think about the wording of the email you are going to send out to get that job interview.

You have to send out lots and lots of emails to get a job interview.

The more email letters you send, the greater will be your chances of having several job interviews.

So, set yourself a goal to send out at least one email letter every day to a company. If you send just one email every day, then by the end of the month you will have sent 30 emails.

Let's expect a positive reply of 10%...so we are talking about having 3 companies who will contact you and ask you to come in for an interview.

Here is an email idea you can use:

Dear Warren Smith
I would like to work at XYZ to provide you with new clients for Microsoft Dynamics CRM.

You might want to tell them how you are going to do this....

Here's what I will do to bring in more clients...(who will be interested in buying your products or the service that you offer):

Or

Here is how I will bring in the new software clients:
I will be phoning the key decision makers at companies doing research on the current accounting software they are using.
I will be recording this information into an Accounting Software Database with categories like:
What is the name of the accounting software they are using?
Which version do they have?

How many users are there?
Which modules have they got?
What problems are they having?
From the leads I have generated, I will be setting up appointments for the sales consultants to meet the new clients.
New doors are going to open for XYZ as we go forward to reach new heights and break new sales records.
I look forward to hearing from you.
Warm Regards
Bernard Levine

Or perhaps you would like to send an email that is short and sweet...to the point!

<u>I would like to work at Woodlands</u>
Dear Madam / Sir
I would like to work at Woodlands as a Telemarketer.
Here's what I would like to do at your company:

I would like to fill your diaries with lots of qualified accounting sales appointments.
Or
I would like to provide you with more clients and increase your sales turnover.
I look forward to hearing from you.
Warm Regards
Bernard Levine

Where would you be without any income at all? You don't want to go down that route at all!
Half a loaf is better than no bread at all! Yes, there are times that you have to lower your salary expectations and take whatever salary you get offered.
…at least, even if the salary they offer is way below what you really want, this low salary, although not to your liking will still be much better than at the end of the month having no income at all to bring home.

I know that by taking a lower salary you might not be able to meet all your monthly commitments and responsibilities, but the money you receive could just be the difference between survival mode and being utterly destitute.

One of the most important things to consider is you might not like doing the job they are offering you, but for the meantime you've got to put food on the table and be able to live.

If you can't find the job you actually want and like, instead of just declining that job offer and sitting at home doing nothing, take the work they give you and use the opportunity you have to add to your experience ....and then while you are at the company earning an income, you will be able to look around until you can find something better, more to your liking with a better salary than you are now receiving.

You've got to persevere….you must not give up.
If you get rejected, so what! There are plenty fish out in the sea…as the song goes…it's all about picking yourself up, dusting yourself off and starting all over again!

How to get Job interviews

It's a connections game....Who are your connections?
It's not what you know...it's who you know.
You've got to reach out and spread your wings to meet new contacts....you've got to widen your circle of contacts.
Try joining Networking Groups, or go attend business breakfasts...also make a list of friends, neighbours, family members who could introduce you to their business contacts and connections.

Make a list of 100 people you know or influential contacts.
Who's your hairdresser?...and your doctor and dentist?
Who are your children's teachers?
Who lives across the road from you?
Who do you know at your church?
Who goes to the same Gym as you?
What's the name of the owner or manager of your local supermarket?
What's the name of your Vet?
Who services your car?
Very soon you will see your list of contacts expanding greatly and very soon you will have your Top 100 names who could perhaps help you or tell you who to contact using their name as a referral.

How do most people go about getting a job?
Everybody is doing the same thing!
They all just post their CV on several job websites, or they go for interviews and

leave their CV at a number of Employment Personnel Agencies hoping for the best! …and most times, that's where it stays and nothing happens! Many of the staff working in Human Resources Departments or at Personnel Agencies just don't care. They treat you like a number and as soon as you leave their office, your file is placed right at the bottom of the pile or stored away in the draw and then they attend to the next in line job candidate…'Next please!'

You've got to stand out from the rest of the pack.
You've got to make your mark and be remembered!
How do you do this?
I don't believe that you should just talk and carry on talking at your interview.
It is very boring hearing someone rambling on and on.

Go buy yourself a flip-file….it's a file that has lots of see-through plastic sleeves.

What you are going to do is 'Show & Tell'!

One of the big secrets of success is preparation!

The more you prepare, the luckier you will get!

This 'Show & Tell' file is going to be your 'Achievement File' for your prospective Employer to get to know you better.

If you have any copies of Diplomas or Degrees, put them inside the plastic sleeves of this file.

If you are married, insert a photo of your partner into one of the sleeves in the file. Let your future Employer get to know you…much more than your CV can say, let them see your life story in pictures.

Because every picture tells a story and one picture is worth more than a thousand words.

Show them a photo of your house.. that is only if you feel it will leave a good impression...otherwise don't have this photo in your file.

Place a copy of your ID Document in the file.

Do you have any newspaper clippings about yourself?...School or sporting achievements etc

Are you a member of any professional organization, or club memberships...you might like to show them these photos or certificates.

To have greater visual impact, only use colour photo copies in your file.

It's all about likeability and trust.

You've got to make them like you and trust you.

They've got to feel comfortable in your company.

You've got to make them want you by telling them what you can offer....what you are able to do at the company.
Please set yourself a goal to contact at least 3 companies every day.
After you have contacted, and gone personally to meet the decision makers at between 20 and 30 companies, clearly identifying what you are able to do for them, you will find that the odds will be very much in your favour for you to have several job proposals that you will be able to choose from.

When you call, give them an alternative:

Would you prefer seeing me in the beginning of the week or the latter part of the week?
Would you prefer a morning appointment or an afternoon appointment?

Have you considered working for yourself?

Sometimes the job market and the circumstances surrounding the job market are not favourable and even after you have tried and tried, you still may not have succeeded in finding a job.

With your priority and main purpose of urgently needing to get a regular monthly income to provide for your daily living expenses and necessities, the right solution might be for you to start your own business.

But you may ask, how can I start my own business without having any money?

There are a number of businesses you can start with either having no money at all or with a minimal cash outlay.

Let's look at some of the businesses you can start:

Can you cut hair? ….start your own men's hairdressing salon from your home.

A garden service…somebody I know took his lawnmower, spade, fork and rake and went door-to-door to homes in his neighbourhood.

And today…he sits at home answering the phone for his garden service business, while his team of 12 drivers with their gardeners are busy cleaning up company gardens.

Baby sitting service

Home tutoring providing extra lessons in maths, science, language lessons to name a few subjects you might consider doing.

School shuttle service….fetching and taking children to school, ballet, karate, swimming lessons, etc

Care giver....providing a service to retirement villages and old age homes taking the residents to shopping centres, doctor's appointments, hairdressers ...

Small parcel and letter delivery service
Selling garden pot plants to businesses
Cooking and baking classes
Looking after pets
Entertaining at children's parties
Having a flea market stall for the crafts you make
Dress making and tailoring
Using your voice, narrating
Translating from one language to another
Teaching magic to children
Teaching pupils how to play a musical instrument like guitar, piano or singing lessons
Homework supervision
Teaching people to draw or paint...art classes
Massage and reflexology
Painting owner's homes
House cleaning service especially new homes before the buyers take occupation
Start your own Estate Agency sales and rentals

Have your own community newspaper
Pool cleaning
Carpentry and home improvements
Making Signs
Printing
Wedding planner
Spring cleaning service
Car valet
Photography especially attending sporting events at schools and also school photography
Wedding photography
Company news letters

Pet grooming

Antique and Collectibles Dealer

Book and Magazine Dealer

Apartment Locator

Debt Collection Agency

Computer Tutor for Children

Online copywriter

Correspondence Club

Dating and Escort Service

Directory Publisher

Employment Agency

Errand Service

Gift Basket Business

Magic at children's birthday parties

Food Delivery Service

Freelance Photographer

Freelance Writer

Make your own greeting cards for sale

Babysitting and day care

Baking/cooking start an online shop

Photography lessons

Web programming

Computer repair

Social media consulting

Fitness instruction

Write slogans for companies

Life coaching

Beauty consultations

- Clean homes
- Invitation printing
- Matchmaker service
- Print merit and award certificates
- Newsletter publishing
- Newspaper clipping service
- Personalized stationery
- Photography family portraits, animals, children, events
- Make custom wooden furniture
- Sell advertising
- Bookkeeping

Yoga Facilitator

Teach dance classes

Make and sell baby blankets

Sell handmade jewellery

Printing Broker

Printer toner recharging

Personalised invitations

Proof-reader

Real estate magazine

Real Estate Agent

Sell bottled water at events

Reporter

Rubber stamps for businesses

Voice over artist

Apartment preparation service

Telemarketing

Using your car or van to make money

Sell flower arrangements

Start an office cleaning company

Home cleaning

Make your own sauces and sell at flea markets

Make and sell birdhouses and bird feeders

Make scratch boards and tunnels for cats

Last minute accommodation

Writing press releases

Start a list of Properties to rent in your area

Start an area newspaper and sell advertising

Sell plastic, cardboard, newspapers, metal, bottles, cans

Sell celebrity autographed photos (which you get for free) to restaurants and interior decorators.

Baby sitting service

Sell your own bottled pickles and cultured foods

List of holiday homes to rent

Put poetry onto trays, mirrors

Print or make and sell car-signs

Taxi Service for seniors, children and everyone

Look for car manuals to sell

Sell second hand toys

Sell sheet music manuscripts

Paint and sell pine cones as Christmas decorations

Find sterling silver at charity shops and sell on Ebay

Look for vintage watches to sell

Sell porcelain

Vinyl records sell on Ebay

Sell corporate gifts

Advertise your own business on websites where you don't have to pay, make signs to put up on notice boards or free advertising in your local community newspapers...put signs up at the public library, restaurants, take-away outlets, the church notice board and where ever there is a constant flow of people who will see your posters.
Search and go through all your belongings in your cupboards. See what you have that you don't want or don't

use any more, items that you can sell that will bring in quick cash.

And most important of all…please don't forget to pray!
Very often, we try too hard in our own strength.
You've got to 'let go and let God' take over your life.
Ask God to open doors and lead you to the right opportunities and bring the right people into your life.

Look to Jesus for Your Victory

When your heart is broken
When your world is tumbling down
Whatever you are going through
I want you to know

God will deliver you
and everything is going to be all right
Your path may seem unclear right now
but soon you will see
that God's mighty power
will let you have your victory
So praise Him in the storm
Praise Him in the trial
Live one day at a time
and the miracle you so long for
will suddenly come to be!

There's a new world just around the corner waiting to unfold especially for you.
There are lots of wonderful gifts, miracles and wonders coming your way but nothing will happen until you make it happen.

Happiness and success are what you make happen for yourself!

Advice for your Job Interview

Start your day with a good positive attitude.
Dress for success.... always dress formally portraying a professional image.
Before going to a job interview, the best you can do is prepare and anticipate some answers to the questions they might ask you.
'Tell me about yourself.'
Give them <u>only</u> positive feedback...don't complain and moan...all the bad things that have happened to you in the past is not their business, and besides they are not really interested.
Think why you are there?

You've come to get a job...you have to impress and convince them...you are not there to tell them about your problems. They are looking for positive people who can contribute and be an asset to the company...what they are not looking for is misery and a 'woe is me' attitude. Leave your problems at home...don't bring it to your job interview.
Tell them about your best achievements and personal attributes.
'Why do you want to work at our company?'

Make sure you do research on each company on the internet prior to visiting them.
And before going for your interview, you must prepare how you are going to answer this question if it comes up.
You might want to tell them that you see their company as being a market leader and you think highly of them.

Try to arrive at your interview at least 10 minutes before your appointment.

Put a smile on your face.

Impress the recruiter with your skills

Don't take your friends, family or one of your parents along to the interview ...this might leave the impression that you are insecure and cannot make decisions for yourself.

Switch off your cell phone before the interview. If your phone rings, this will interrupt the proceedings of your interview and may spoil your chances of getting a job.

Avoid all negative conversation...let your speech be positive displaying a good attitude.

Be friendly and warm.

You've got to set the vibe...you've got to create the right mood, the right atmosphere.

Be confident and remain positive.

If they sense from the way you carry yourself that you are worried, or tense ....this does not leave them with a good impression and it won't encourage them to present you with a job offer.
Believe in yourself and believe in the power of God.

<u>SHOW YOUR LOVE TO GOD</u>

<u>To God Be The Glory</u>

To have a deep hunger for God

and love Him as much as we can

To delight ourselves in the study of His Word

To put Jesus first in our lives

and worship God with praise and joy

To humble ourselves before His throne

and give to God

the highest honour, respect and glory

Always.

Make God your treasure

Your Miracle Is About to Begin

When God wanted a woman to give birth to His son

He didn't choose a prominent girl

but God found favour in an ordinary woman called Mary.

When God needed a new king for Israel

He could have chosen someone distinguished

but God chose an ordinary shepherd boy called David.

When Jesus chose His 12 disciples

He didn't choose men who were well educated

but Jesus took ordinary men willing to follow Him.

God takes ordinary people and performs mighty miracles

All you have to do is love God with all your heart

Give God abundant praise and appreciation

and very soon you will see your miracle begin.

Walking in the Power of God

The Bible is the only book

where the Author is present every time we read it!

Faith is like electricity...it is there all the time

and its force and power work!

When you pray, God sends angels.

Get out of begging and into the praising position.

You need God's Word every day to feed you.

Every breath is a miracle.

Be thankful for each day God gives you.

Don't miss the many opportunities you have

to lay up for yourself treasures in heaven.

Keep your eyes on God's power

and your heart on His love.

God searches our hearts

to see just how much we really love Him!

Remember...God's mighty power

is only a prayer away!

Take the bull by the horns and apply the principles I have shared with you in this book and success will be yours!

EXPERT TELEMARKETING

How to urgently get lots of sales appointments

By Bernard Levine

If you are wanting to fill your diary with lots of sales appointments, this unique book will bring you fast guaranteed results.

Let's give you what you want!
You urgently need to get quick sales....like yesterday!
You don't have time to waste.
You want to know where to look to find the right people that you can tell them about the services that you have to offer, show them

your products and walk away with the signed order.

How do you do it?

You don't want to hear about long explanations of how you should talk on the phone.

You also don't want to be bogged down with lots of boring telephone conversation sales scripts for you to wade through.

What you need right now is the fastest way there is to get to see the people and make the sale.

Okay, let's get on with it!

First and foremost who are you going to talk to?

Have you decided, and do you know who your target market is?

You've got to have an audience to tell your story to and present your product.

Decide who your target market is...what type of companies or buyers do you want to sell to?

Who is most likely to buy your product?

What type of occupation would be most interested in what you have to offer?

Which three specific occupations or professions would be interested in your product or service?

Would it be accountants?... electricians? or engineers?

You must decide and choose who you think would be the most likely type of person who would use your product.

Does your product appeal more to women than to men? Or is it more suitable for children?

Once you have established and decided on a specific target market for your product or service, we can look at where to find the right people you need to approach.

How do you find good leads?

There are so many varied and different places where you can look for prospects to phone. Have you ever thought of going through the business pages of your local newspaper to see who has been promoted?

Not only will you find the name and job title of the person who has been promoted, but you will also see the name of the company. Now, all you've got to do is to look up the name of the company in the phone book, or

find the company's name on the internet and then phone and congratulate the person who has been promoted.
Everybody likes a warm friendly greeting and your phone call will be welcome and a good way to start your conversation:
'Good morning John. Congratulations on your new appointment!'

An ideal place where you will find names and occupations of key decision makers are at printing shops where they make business cards.
Go along to a few of these printing companies in the area where you work or live, and ask them to show you some examples of their printed business cards.
They will usually bring out a big box of business cards which they have printed for clients.
Search through the many different cards in the box taking careful note of the company's names as well as the job designation of each person's name on the business cards.
(Of course, you should already have a good idea and know the type of company and the

occupation of the person you would like to phone).

Ask the printer if you could please have some samples of their business cards. They will gladly give you a whole stack of business cards to take away.

You can also try looking at the classified ads in the newspapers. There, you will find more prospects to phone who could be interested in your products or services.

Referrals are an excellent way to get new clients.

Go along, don't be shy...ask your hairdresser to give you a few contact names and phone numbers of their business contacts, friends and family.

How about asking your next-door neighbour or the people living across the road for some names and numbers...and don't forget to ask your local butcher or convenience store.

Also look for business contact names appearing on signs at super markets and public library notice boards, as well as business cards advertising various services that are left on the counter at your local hardware store.

And don't forget to spend time researching on the web to find the specific categories of the companies you are needing, together with the names of the directors and their contact details.

A good starting point in your telemarketing campaign would be to compile a list of 100 appropriate names for you to contact.
Now, we are going to prepare to start phoning your prospects.
What are you going to say?
What is vital?
The most important point is that we are not going to be selling the product over the phone.
Our only goal and our top priority is to phone and get an appointment.
That's all we've got to do!
When you call, don't give away too much information about what you have to sell them.
Keep them intrigued!
The less they know…the better!
If you tell them too much, you are giving them lots of opportunities to find a reason or an excuse why they should not see you.

Then, you will have to waste time handling their objections.

You are most likely to hear common objections like:

'I can't afford it!', 'I'm not interested', 'I have no use for your product', 'First send me an email, then I'll decide', 'We have already completed our budget' and various other excuses to end the conversation.

Please don't bother and waste time arguing with them and trying to convince them why your product or service is an absolute must-have for them.

It really is not worth it! Just hang up and put the phone down...go forward and move on. Remember there are hundreds and thousands of other names that you could phone, so why get yourself all in a knot over someone who doesn't even want to give you a chance to even see what your product can do.

Who should you speak to?

Always go straight to the top...

Speak to the decision-makers in the company like the owner, CEO, Managing Director, Financial Director or General Manager. Don't waste your energy and time speaking to the head of the department or a manager...they don't have the power and authority to make a decision.

It depends on what your company is selling ...if you can, try to offer a free trial version of the product or arrange for them to see a demo.

Receptionists have been told by their bosses to screen all calls.

So, how do you get past the receptionist or switchboard operator?

When you call someone, you must not come across or sound like a salesman on the phone. People are sick and tired of salesmen bothering them.

You've got to have a unique gimmick or a style of your own on the phone.

How you sound and come across in the first 60 seconds of your phone call is absolutely vital.

You've got to set the mood and entertain them.
Be polite, warm and confident.
I am going to give you a secret winning, very unusual telephone approach for you to master....a unique telephone approach that will bring you exceptional success!
It's based on the element of surprise.
The big secret is the receptionist does not expect to receive a phone call like this call that you are about to make....and because it's so very different and not the norm...that's exactly the reason why it works so well!
The receptionist is taken off guard and because she has never received a call like yours before, she does not know how to handle the call.
Remember, you've got to be different and stand out from all the rest of the phone calls that the receptionist receives.
Ring!...Ring!....Ring!
The receptionist answers the phone:
'Good morning Nestle Chocolates....Kathy speaking...How may I direct your call?'
You respond:

'Good morning, I want to speak to that very good looking, adorable, lovable, likeable, intelligent young lady called.....
I didn't get your name.'
(This is very easy to do...it's a mixture of lots of different adjectives that I have put together to fascinate and captivate to grab her attention.
It's even more effective if you practise and say these lines fast...that really gets them going and they like it a lot.)
Why do they like it a lot?
If you think about the daily work and job of the receptionist...every call is usually the same...very routine and mostly very boring.
These are the type of calls the receptionist deals with every day:
'What's the name of your Managing Director? Put me through!'
'Who's in charge of IT department? Put me through!'
The poor receptionist is often abused by the staff at the company and by many of the callers.
At a busy switchboard, the receptionist usually doesn't even get the chance to finish

drinking her coffee and often has difficulty in finding someone to take over her duties on the switchboard so that she can quickly go to the toilet.

The way that some of the callers treat the poor receptionist is extremely rude and very bad...

'You cut me off...I'm going to report you! What's your name?'

Now, when the receptionist answers your phone call, it is going to be totally different. Suddenly, out of the blue comes your phone call, very unusual but so refreshing!

Your phone call is such a welcome break away from all the boring hum-drum phone calls the receptionist gets every day.

The receptionist replies:

'I'm Kathy...who is that? What do you want? Where are you calling from?'

'Hi Kathy, I'm Bernie from Webatar.

Kathy, I need your wisdom, your truth, your love, expertise, professionalism, your help and advice...

Kathy, I need you to hold my hand and point me in the right direction.... please don't squeeze me too hard!'

The receptionist laughs.
'Bernie, you can have everything you've asked for.... how can I help you?'
'Kathy, our company wants to do business with your company....and my boss has asked me to speak to one of your directors or partners to make a short 15 minute to half an hour appointment to see one of your directors.
My boss's name is Malcolm...he wants to find out how you guys operate?... how your company works?... do you charge per hour or per project? so he can know what would be the best way to go forward.'
'Kathy, which director is available now that I can talk to?'

The receptionist answers:
'Okay, I'll put you through to John Royce, he is one of our senior partners...what did you say your name was?... and your company's name?'
'I'm putting you through!'
The director answers:

'Royce, good morning'.
You reply:
'Good morning John Royce. My name is Bernie.
I'm from Webatar. I've been asked to call you by my boss, his name is Malcolm Peterson ....he wants to do business with your company...Malcolm asked me to arrange a short 15 minute to half hour appointment to meet you. The purpose of the meeting is for Malcolm to find out some details such as how you guys operate... and the different services that you offer so he can have a better idea of the way going forward.
John, I don't know if you are a mornings person or an afternoon person?
Would you prefer seeing Malcolm on Tuesday morning, at 10....or would you prefer Wednesday at 2 in the afternoon?
Once you have chosen the day and time you would like,
I'll send you a Microsoft Outlook Invite for you to accept and send back to me.
John, you say you would like to see Malcolm at 10 in the morning on Thursday the 12th

July....I'm looking at Malcolm's diary now and I see that he will be available.
Please may I have your email address so I can send you the invite?
Also John, what is your physical address?
Thank you so much John....I'll send you the meeting request now.
Have a good day!
Bye!'

What is important for you to know?
Dial with a smile.
You've got to create the right mood on the phone.
The tone of your voice must be joyful and happy...make them smile or laugh but don't use slang or say anything rude and definitely no dirty jokes...you must not say anything that will offend. Be friendly and polite. Always give them a choice...let them be able to choose the day and time they prefer...a choice of between one of two different dates.

Telemarketing is a numbers game and the more calls you make, the greater will be your chance of success....

The law of averages will never let you down! Don't sell your product or service on the phone...you must only focus on getting an appointment.

Book short appointments...time is valuable...long appointments are not welcome and are not appealing.

Make short appointments to get your foot in the door.

Confirm the details of the appointment you have made before you go.

Also confirm the address...search for the company's name on the internet.

There's power in sending a 'thank you' letter after you have been to see the client:

Dear Robert

Just a short note to say 'thank you' for seeing me today.
I really enjoyed talking to you.
I will prepare a new revised quote to send to you tomorrow morning.
Warm Regards
Bernie

What questions should you ask?

There are two different types of questions...open-ended questions and closed-ended questions.

What's the difference between a closed question and an open question?

When you begin your question with any one of the following words, you are asking an open question:

How?
Why?
Where?
When?
Which?
What?

Open questions are good to ask, because it gets them to talk more, explaining and answering in greater detail.

Closed questions will have a short reply of either:
Yes!
No!
Maybe!
Perhaps!
Possible!

If you want a quick short answer, then ask questions that begin with any one of the following words:

Do?
Can?
Could?
Will?
Are?
Should?
May?
Is?
Have?
Would?
Shall?
Did?
Does?

Here are some additional questions you could ask:

'Would you like seeing Malcolm in the beginning of the week or the latter part of the week?'

'Would you rather prefer coming to our offices?'

'What is the name of the product that you are currently using?'

'Which version?'

'What problems are you experiencing?'

'What would you like the product to do for you?'

'Are you involved in the …. industry?'

'Would it help if we could show you a less expensive….?'

'Are you using ….?'

'Have you given thought to the problems you are actually having and the costs you have to incur?'

'How do you deal with….?'

'Is this a problem for your company?'

'Can we give you a solution to meet your budget and requirements? We will save you money and huge costs.'
'Would you like to see a free demo of Webatar?'
'If I can give you..... would you be interested?'
'Are you finding the cost of .....very expensive?'
'Have you ever had to call in a .....to sort out problems you were having?'

In this world, it doesn't matter what people think of
you...
the only thing that matters is what God thinks of you.

Get paid for the poems you write

By Bernard Levine

Do you love writing poems?

Now, you can get paid for the poetry you write and have your poems published in greeting cards, calendars, posters and wall-plaques.

If you want to make your writing dreams come true and get cash for your poetry, this unique book is especially for you.

Here's the inside information from Bernard Levine, a Greeting Card writer for more than 30 years of how you too, can get paid.
Find all your old romantic verse which you have written and let's get your poetry published with money in your Bank account! Writing poems for cash is a whole lot of fun and very profitable! **Get paid doing what you love.**

Anybody can send their rhymes or poems to publishers who pay $300 when they're used in a greeting card.

Publishers of greeting cards are always looking for one-liner slogans and short verse which they can use to publish in their greeting cards and they are willing to pay you handsomely for your original work.

There is a secret of how to get your poems accepted and published by Greeting Card Companies....if you send them your poems, you most likely will be rejected. Why?

Because there are specific things that Greeting Card Companies would like you to do before they accept and publish your work.

So you've written a love poem…how much will you get paid for it?

What are the rules of getting published by Card Companies. How do you go about it?

Okay! Let's get started…..Rule Number 1 is 'How Long Is Your Poem?
Make sure that your poem is no longer than 12 lines absolute maximum…..in fact, if you can make your verse to be even shorter, so much the better.
Greeting Card Companies don't want long boring poems….the buyers of Greeting Cards have not got the time to stand in the shop and read long boring poetry.

Here's Rule Number 2…..How will I feel after I have read your poem?

Greeting Card Companies are not looking for sad, uninspiring writing. Nobody is going to pay for poetry that is sad and leaves them feeling blue and depressed.

Your message must either be fun to read or it must convey positive, happy feel-good spirit. If your verse isn't humorous then it should be uplifting to the reader.

Here's an example of verse that offers encouragement and motivation:

PRECIOUS
By Bernard Levine

**If you ever need
A helping hand in this world
If ever you need
Someone to understand
I'm the one who loves you
I'm the one who cares
If you ever need
A friend
Just know
I'll be there!**

You should focus on love poems that are **positive, romantic, and easy to understand**. Here's another example of verse that doesn't rhyme, but the message flows leaving you with a feeling of warmth, sincerity and love:

JUST FOR YOU
By Bernard Levine

Darling
I dedicate my love to you
to make your life more beautiful
Your love means everything to me
Your smile makes my world brighter
Your kiss awakens my soul
Your touch is a very special magic
Baby, Take me in your arms
and let me love you!

Some of the most popular greeting card occasions are:
Birthday
Valentines Days
Mother's Day
Father's Day
Wedding
Engagement
Anniversary
Thank You
Graduation
Christmas

Can you think of any other times, special occasions, events and celebrations when it would be nice to send someone a unique message?

Think about moments of friendship, family, hope, encouragement, love, life, happiness, success, positive living and other topics one person might want to share with another person.

What type of greeting cards do the stores not have?

Here are some themes and ideas you can write about....
Well done! you've lost so much weight and it looks absolutely great!
Thank you for giving me a precious little baby.
My 3 wishes.
Meet me in your dreams tonight.
Step right into my life.
Make me know that I'm wanted, make me know that you care.
I want to share your world.
My happiness is you, my love.

A UNIQUE WAY FOR YOU TO MAKE MONEY SELLING YOUR VERSE, ONE LINERS AND SLOGANS IS HAVING

YOUR WORDS PRINTED ON GIFT PRODUCTS.

You will love the following websites where you can submit your words and you can choose which products you would like to have your poetry printed on. They will manufacture, promote and sell your products featuring your words and you will be rewarded with a good income.

Your poetry will be printed on gift products like:
Place-mats, coasters, T-shirts, aprons, mirrors, wall hangings, fridge magnets, posters, calendars, bookmarks, diaries, coffee mugs, mouse-pads, trays, wall-tiles, scatter cushions, words for scrap-books and even teddy bear bibs!

www.cafepress.com   They have a huge range of products for your words.

www.zazzle.com   They will promote your words on their products with passion!

FROM THE HEART

Darling

I love being with you.

You inspire me to achieve my ambitions

You fill my world with surprises

I feel I have found a new life.

In my mind you are adorable

In my heart you are completeness

I am yours totally

In support

Through all our tomorrows.

IF I COULD BE

If I could be ...

The sun shining down on your face

The soft breeze blowing through your hair

If I could be ...

The ring you wear on your hand

The food you taste and bite

The spot where you sit or stand

The blanket that covers you at night.

If I could only be ...

There are more than 3,000 greeting card publishers in America.

Here's a few greeting card publishers where you can submit your words:

Blue Mountain Arts

American Greetings

Hallmark

Oatmeal Studios

Kalan

PS Greetings

Dayspring

Avanti Press

Papyrus Design

Broom Designs

Gallant Greeting Corp

Novo Card Publishers

Ephemera, Inc

Moonlighting Cards

The Great British Card Company

Comstock Cards

Here's some useful information about writing greeting cards:

Greeting Card Association

Writers Write

Greeting Card Writing Tip Sheet

Mom
By Bernard Levine

You are our mother,
friend,
guide,
taxi-service,
money-lender,
date-finder,
dictionary,
time-keeper,
message-bureau
and no one
Can ever take your place!

Dedication

To my precious wife, Chrissie thank you so much for all your love and kindness.

To Whiskers (Wikkie), Maggie Mae, Bo Peep, Benji and Stewart Little you give me so much joy.

Copyright

All rights reserved under International Copyright Law.

No part of this book may be reproduced or transmitted in any form or by any means, electronic or mechanical, including photocopying, recording, or by any information storage and retrieval system, without the written permission of the author.

©Bernard Levine 2020

About Bernard Levine

Bernard Levine is the author of 47 published books on sale both locally and internationally at more than 700 bookstores.

Bernard's books have been translated into 12 languages and are also available as Audio-books.

Awesome Love
Hidden Secrets of the Jewish World Now Revealed
Passionately Praise Jesus
What would you do for the one you love?
Who took the name of God out of the Bible?
100's of Opportunities for you to make money
How to witness to Jews about

Jesus...what Christians need to know

You are not supposed to know the Secrets of the Jews (Secrets of the Jewish World) (Volume 3)

Intimate Sex Secrets of the Jews

The Best of Bernard Levine

The Secrets of the Jews: (What Christians don't know about the Jewish religion, traditions and way of life)

How to find a job quickly and easily

Make money collecting books, get free celebrity autographs and more!

Expert Telemarketing: How to Urgently Get Lots of Sales Appointments

The Secrets of the Jewish World (What Christians don't know about the Jewish religion, traditions and way of life Book 1)

- Why I left the Jewish religion to follow Jesus
- How to meet your soul mate: There is someone very special waiting to meet you
- There Is Nothing to Pay!: Get It All for Free...
- Meet Freddy the friendly Fireman
- How to please your loved one (in 100 different ways): The magic of romantic love
- Children love Nursery Rhymes
- Children love to tell jokes
- Get paid for the poems you write
- How To Receive Your Miracle
- The Fun Conversation Book
- Change Your Destiny
- A Book Full of Wonderful Exciting Surprises
- Meet Tommy the funny Toy Maker

How to get paid appearing in TV Ads and Soapies

The Secrets of Life: Inspiration you will never forget!

FUN By The TON!

Make money collecting everyday easy to find items

The World's Best Loved Inspiration

Save the Jews: What Jewish people do not know about Jesus

Do you remember?: All the fun stuff is here!

Children Love to Sing: Teach your children the songs you sang when you were a child

How to make your life more exciting

You can never say 'Thank You' enough to Jesus

The Jewish Confidential Files never published before!

When you pray, God sends angels

Did you live? Did you love? Did it matter?
Darling, I want you to know how very special you are to me
Have you heard there are going to be prizes handed out in heaven?
What would you do if you saw Jesus?

The Bernard Levine Christian Library

Your Favorite Bernard Levine Christian Books

How to Get Paid and Start Earning a Good Income

www.ingramcontent.com/pod-product-compliance
Lightning Source LLC
Chambersburg PA
CBHW020645220526
45464CB00001B/297